Frazzle to Dazzle

How to *not* Be a Victim
of an Inexperienced Hairdresser

Tricia Greenwood

Cover Design: Tricia Greenwood
Photo on back cover by Mel Lindstrom
Publisher: Heartspeak Publishing
Editor: Hamilton Wordsworth
Creative Consultant: Heather Haven
Library of Congress Control Number: 2016912813
ISBN: 978-0-9978798-0-3
Printed in USA

I dedicate this book to you...

*I believe in living in love, faith and hope
because I have seen miracles happen. I believe
God gave me a heart filled with compassion that
has endured much. Whatever I choose to do, it is
with the desire to make others happy and more
beautiful.*

*Hairdressers are a wonderful breed.
You work one-on-one with another human being
and the object is to make them feel so much better
and to look at themselves with a twinkle in their eye.*
-Vidal Sassoon

Contents

INTRODUCTION

The looking glass we gaze into each day reflects how the rest of the world perceives us. At the present time, a large percentage of our social interactions are conducted with our electronic devices and computers. This enables us all to communicate with each other on social networks like Facebook, Twitter, Linkedin and others that serve as portals for personal networking, employment and even dating.

These networks have one particular feature in common that is necessary to be recognized and acknowledged: our Image. One that has our face and yes… our *hair* as our identity.

Looking your best is important for a first impression online and in person. It's not a matter of being vain, but a matter of courtesy and professionalism. Think about how great you feel when you look your best by projecting a positive, confident self-image.

In chapter five you will discover what type of style will look best on your facial shape and how to successfully communicate with your Hair Designer.

Chapter seven covers all you need to know about hair color products for the best outcome. There are new smoothing and straightening services available to keep your hair in the best condition. Learn the difference between permanents and body waves, including the new chemical free products available today that I have personally tested.

You will appreciate some "behind the scene scenarios" that are true stories.

My wish is that this book will forever change your future encounters with hair services and salon experiences in general. By sharing important information, you to be able to communicate on a higher level. You will be empowered to remain the author or the co-author of your hair design as applied to your Image.

Chapter eight will give you a whole new perspective on *inner beauty* - The kind that lasts!

Foreword

"To be a leader of one's career, one first has to gather the knowledge and experience of others, act according to the facts and logic, that should prevail through the understanding of the core values that we all share as Artistic Engineer (hairdressers, stylists, cosmetologists, crimpers and designers). Reading this book gives commonality that we all share. Well done Tricia."
- Alan Benfield Bush

Chapter 1
Everyone's Got a Story

I want to say that I truly admire great Hair Designers in the beauty profession and I love surrounding myself with the best.

I wrote this book to help you, "the client" better understand how to achieve results you desire in regard to your haircut or hairstyle. My goal is to help you have better communication on all levels regarding the services you request at a salon.

A professional Hair Designer will understand and possess the knowledge, experience and ability to cut and color your hair with complete confidence in knowing the outcome.

Art is subjective and each Hair Designer has their own techniques that they execute to create their clients' individual unique hairstyle.

> *"The best and most beautiful things*
> *in the world cannot be seen or even touched –*
> *they must be felt with the heart."*
> *- Helen Keller*

Although there are proven methods, modern techniques and excellent products available today, not every professional stylist employs them all.

I have found that there is a lack of knowledge in the hair industry largely because accredited beauty schools are only required to prepare students for the state board exam in each state.

It is not the fault of the instructor at any given beauty school, it's just that advanced education is required for the student to be confident in what they are doing once they graduate.

Professionals that are licensed to use scissors like (Doctors or Surgeons) usually have to complete an internship before they are approved and licensed to work in their state.

In all US states, Cosmetology instructors use the same standard book to teach the students lessons in haircutting, hairstyling and hair color. I know from my own experience as well as having been told by others that when students ask a question regarding certain practical techniques, their beauty school instructor informs them that they will get answers to these questions in their salon experience once they graduate and are hired to do hair in the "real world".

My younger sister, "Francine" recently graduated from a beauty college in Florida. She likes it when I tell people she is younger.

She told me the same story I have heard for years… when a client comes into her beauty school for a cut or color, a consultation with the instructor and student is performed together. After the

11

consultation, the color service is determined and the instructor informs the student to prepare the client with a drape and towel. The instructor then mixes the hair color formula for the client's hair and returns, giving the bowl of color formula to the student to apply.

Here's the problem... the student has no knowledge of what is *in* the formula she is applying on the client's head! The student is being supervised to apply the color formula correctly for a retouch by dividing the hair into four sections and using a brush or bottle to apply to the roots of the client's hair at the scalp.

For the practical test, the state board exam only requires the student to be graded on his or her knowledge of the application of the product. During the exam, instead of hair color, a hair conditioner is used for the formula. This raises questions rarely answered at this stage of learning.

The truth is... being mentored and receiving advanced education is a must for graduates from beauty school. Simply going to hair shows will *not* be enough to be trained properly.

If you know anyone in beauty school, make them aware that there are schools and workshops like the one Alan Benfield Bush has available. As a former Director for Vidal Sassoon, Alan has developed his precision art as, "The Method" having mastered the art of cutting in terms easy to learn and understand.

Currently, Vidal Sassoon School has a five-day course for licensed hairdressers and JBeverly Hills has a weekend cutting academy in Beverly Hills. Also, there is a Mastercutter Academy you can find online. Also, Toni & Guy have advanced education. Ask your hairdresser if they may have heard of any of them.

Perhaps you are one of the millions of people who have been a victim of inexperienced hairdressers or you may be someone who would like to overcome your fear of becoming a victim.

You may be a client, a student or a hairdresser that simply needs more communication skills.

I decided to write this book for a number of reasons. When I first started out wanting to become a Hair Designer, I met a hairdresser in Sunnyvale,

California. His name was Ty Mighetto, a handsome Italian guy whose father, Eddie Mighetto in his youth had been Frank Sinatra's personal barber for years. I heard many stories when I went to his classy shop called, "The Particular Man".

Women also had their hair cut there and Ty taught me the techniques of haircutting. I had learned enough from Ty about cutting and styling hair to do it for friends as well as cutting my own hair.

Before I went to cosmetology school I had an interesting experience in Buffalo, New York.

One exciting night at the Executive dinner nightclub I was working as a dinner server in a tux jacket with black tights, a ruffled blouse, black bow tie and black pumps. Chateaubriand was the top seller on the menu and it was a dinner nightclub scene like in the classic movies. The entertainment was top notch. That night the Monkees were performing on a national tour making a comeback and the place was packed.

So many things took place on this crazy night, including dancing the bump with Davey Jones at the

747 Club, that was an airplane cut in half attached to the building of the Executive Hotel. Davey was shorter than me, he was a great dancer and very sweet. I ended up later cutting both guitar players' hair in their hotel room at the after party all in good fun. Yes, I always carry scissors.

Earlier that evening while the dinner show kept the crowd entertained, I was dodging the spotlights by the stage, delivering cocktails.

A man that resembled Warren Beatty stopped me in my tracks and lightly grabbed my wrist. As I steadied my tray in my other hand he said, "Don't I know you?"
I replied, "I don't think so"
As I turned to walk away he said,
"Wait, who does your hair?"
I said, "I do."
Smiling as he looked at me he asked,
"Are you a hairdresser?"
I said, "Yes, I know how to cut hair but I'm not licensed yet."

He gave me his business card and told me to call him.

I figured maybe this was going to be an opportunity that only knocks once. The next day I called him and he invited me to come over to see his salon.

He seemed desperate to talk to me. When I asked him the name of his salon, he said, "Oh, it's called Shampoo". I thought I was going to die!

A few days later I met him at his salon. It was decorated in red and white with silver accent, located downstairs in a large white business building. His name was Ross and he really *did* look like Warren Beatty. He told me his story about being in a terrible car accident leaving him with burnt nerve endings in his lower back.

At the same time his salon partner had left him owing money and he couldn't run the business at all without him. His plan was to have me run his salon and cut hair for his clients.

Ross had an assistant named Beth. He trained her to shampoo, apply color and roll perms for his clients. She would be able to assist me as well. All I would have to do was cut and style.

Ross offered me his clientele and management of his salon. I wanted to help him as crazy as it sounded and I thought the experience gained would help me in the future. I was young and very naive. I didn't think I would get in too much trouble.

My first client at the salon was an Elvis impersonator I had met who worked at the Executive club with me. He had really fine blonde hair. For his show he would spray his hair with a can of black hair color like one would use for Halloween.

He asked me about giving him a body perm for more fullness and I agreed it would look great.

I knew Beth (my assistant) could help me out. Well, let me tell you, that was a huge mistake!

I found out the world of perms and body waves is not one to be guessed at. After Beth rolled his hair on pink rods, he had a modified bozo perm. He literally freaked out.

He couldn't believe it was his hair in the mirror! He kept looking in the mirror and ducking down in the salon chair like it really wasn't him. Luckily, he had a great sense of humor.

I asked him to come back in for a treatment using a straightening solution to smooth it out. I combed some straightening product through his hair slowly and firmly with a fine tooth comb, it helped straighten out the tight frizzy curls from the pink perm rods that Beth, the assistant used.

The condition of his hair became dry and dull, so I applied a deep conditioning treatment and offered him many free salon treatments in the future. The condition of his hair got much better within weeks. What a lesson I learned that day! After three weeks in that salon, I was ready to quit.

One day I was walking down Main Street in Buffalo and I met up with a substitute teacher I had back in seventh grade. He asked me how I was doing. We stopped in a café for some coffee and I shared with him some hardships about my life since junior high of having to go on my own at sixteen and losing both my parents by the time I was eighteen. I told him I really wanted to go to beauty school.

He told me he was working with a city program to help people get grants for education and if I could pass an IQ test with a high score, he could help me get into a good school. I was so excited!

I made an appointment to take the test and scored high enough to choose the top beauty school in the city. Which I did! It was Peter Piccolo's School for Hair Design, an accredited school teaching Vidal Sassoon and Pivot Point training. Teaching students to see, think and create as a *designer of hair*.

The school curriculum included Redkin Laboratory's intense study of hair under the microscope, called Trichoanalysis, a scientific hair analysis system to study hair.

I excelled in school and after three hundred hours of learning I was asked to cut and style hair in Peter Piccolo's Hair Salon at another location away from the school. I was making money for the salon and great tips for me. I liked the on-the-job training in the "real world" as it was referred to in beauty school.

I knew how to cut and style and it came easy for me so I would cut some of the student's hair from beauty school at my apartment. I was having a great time until it got me in trouble with the director of the school.

She called me into her office and admonished me. She threatened to expel me if I did not *stop* cutting student's hair at my apartment outside of school and the salon. I was crazy about cutting and I still am, but I became a bit more discreet after that episode. I was a bit of a rebel in my younger years.

There was a student at the school named Michelle, who was ready to graduate and she was considered by most to be the best hair cutter in school.

She and I went to a music concert at Buffalo State University together. We got there early for the concert, and while we were in the women's restroom Michelle was looking in the mirror and complaining that the top of her hair was too long.

I pulled out my scissors and she turned over the empty small black trash can so she could sit on it and I cut the top of her hair right there.

It gave me confidence to have her trust me at such an early stage of my education.

Finally, the day came for me to graduate from beauty school; the usual protocol was to have a little celebration before receiving a certificate of completion in order to take the state board exam. There I was on my last day patiently waiting and five o'clock came and everybody left. I asked the director if I was really graduating that day and she apologized while handing me my certificate, shook my hand and said good-bye. (Ouch?)

Although this might have put a little dent in my self-confidence, I knew a few salon owners in Buffalo that liked to have me cut their hair and it gave me a level of confidence that overshadowed that incident. These things can (and will) happen as life's journey unfolds, but it wasn't going to be enough to spoil my accomplishments.

I always try to have a positive attitude and keep my thoughts higher by filling myself with light… it's better then giving in to negativity.

Considering the brutal Buffalo weather, I decided to

return to California with my three-year-old son Jamie James. I spent my teen years in San Jose with my mother before she passed away and I missed my friends there. I loved being near the ocean and the mountains.

As it turned out, I had to take six hundred more hours of Cosmetology school in order to complete training for the CA state board exam. I chose to go to Westgate Beauty School.

When my main instructor found out about my completion of one thousand hours for the New York State Cosmetology certification, she asked me to cut her hair in front of the class. I also gave a theory class to the students on perms. Imagine that...I love to teach!

Later, I transferred to Mountain View Beauty School. At the completion of six hundred hours, the whole class pitched in and bought me a gold bracelet and had it engraved with, "Shear Wizard". I still have it.

Speaking of shear wizards...I had the pleasure of meeting Paul Mitchell at a private hair show in

California where he was demonstrating his new curved scissors. I was very impressed with him and after the show I went up to the stage to meet him. When he looked over at me, I said, "You cut hair just like I do." He laughed and said, "I love it!" I told him I curved my fingers to cut the hair like he did with the new curved scissors. It was a memorable experience.

In memory, the late Horst Rechelbacher was the greatest contributor to my passion for natural hair products. I would like to share an experience I had in Houston, Texas where I met him. He was the founder of Aveda, on a tour through the country giving private salon classes introducing Aveda products along with Jon English, a talented and innovative Hair Designer from the UK.

While I was working at a salon in Houston called, "Joseph Kemble's Scissor Wizards" Horst and Jon arrived to teach all who attended about the benefits of Aveda hair care. Horst had a bit of a cold and I could see he was under the weather. I was sitting at the back of the room and snuck out the side door to get him some orange juice at the market next door. He really appreciated it when I offered it to him.

Years later I saw Horst at a few shows and asked him if I could endorse his products in this book (which I was only *thinking* of writing at the time) and he gave me an enthusiastic "yes". Today, Estee Lauder owns the company.

There are a lot more related experiences through the years but it's time I share the stories of others.

Having met and worked on thousands of clients, I've been licensed in three states and owned a few salons. I decided to specialize in corrective hair color to care for clients dealing with the stress of having their hair ruined by their own doing or by an inexperienced hairdresser.

I feel it's important to share my knowledge with you, because after going to Cosmetology school and passing the state board exams in both New York and CA., it still took years to understand hair color theory and various styling and cutting techniques.

I have witnessed with my own eyes and heard the stories of their awful experiences, and they have given me permission to share them with you.

Chapter 2
Victims of Inexperienced Hairdressers

Ninety percent of hairdressers are women, the rest are men and there are those who really aren't sure themselves.

With all due respect to all Hairdressers, Hairstylists, Hair Designers, Beauty Operators, Barbers, etc., I am sharing these stories to educate with knowledge, experience and compassion for the clients.

All of these stories are unfortunately true - with real victims of inexperienced hairdressers simply due to lack of education and communication.

I apologize if anything I have written in this book offends you or anyone you know (or want to forget).

Sarah saw an advertisement online for a special deal at a price she could afford. She made an appointment and arrived at a new modern salon in her neighborhood. When she arrived the hairdresser walked up and introduced herself.

"Hello, I'm Nadia, will you follow me please?"

Sarah followed her over to her salon chair and sat down explaining, "I have always colored my own hair, I saw the special deal and I am interested in getting high-lights since I'm over fifty. I would like to camouflage my gray. What do you think?"
The hairdresser replied, "No problem!"

She disappeared into the back room for a long time and returned with three bowls of different hair color. While applying the different formulas with a brush to weaved out hair sections on foil, she was looking unsure of which ones to use. (Sarah's natural hair color was almost black with about 30 percent gray.)

Three hours later, the stylist removed all the foils and the highlights had lightened to a brassy gold.

The stylist again disappeared into the back room and returned to the shampoo bowl explaining she had to apply a bleach cap to Sarah's whole head of hair, hoping to help lighten her hair to get rid of the brassiness.

The hairdresser said, "Sarah, your hair is really stubborn, you will also need a toner, and I want to let you know there will be an extra charge."

Twenty-five minutes later the stylist apologizes, "Sarah, that toner was ineffective and I have to apply another one. No charge for the second one."

About five hours later, Sarah walks out confused and starved. Not to mention feeling ripped off. With her hair looking like a two-tone yellow cotton candy doo! Welcome to the twilight zone.... another victim of unskilled and inexperienced hairstylists with hair color.

As I mentioned earlier, beauty schools breed graduates who pass the state board exam without the knowledge needed to perform hair color services in the salon. Most of the students go through school without doing their lab work.

I ended up living in Houston, Texas for almost seven years. One Friday night I was invited out to a comedy show with a few friends. A female comedian walked out on the stage with the most bizarre hairstyle. She was very funny without uttering a word.

Then she spoke, "… Oh yea, well you're all out there probably wondering where I got my hair cut!

Well, actually it was right here in town. I won't mention the name of the place I went to that did this to my hair, but I *will* tell you how it happened.

The concierge at the hotel where I am staying told me about this really cool jungle looking salon. He said, " It's where I get my hair cut." I said "OK". "I looked at his head and noticed he didn't have any hair, only heavy side burns! I guess they shaved his head for him. I desperately needed a trim before the show, so I went anyway.

There I was, sitting next to stuffed monkeys, tree plants and waterfalls in a salon decorated in a jungle motif. I looked around feeling a bit nervous when a woman walked up to me dressed like the road warrior's girlfriend. She was extremely self-confident. I thought to myself, "Okay, there must be a hidden camera somewhere!"

She led me to the back of the salon where I told her I just wanted a trim. After a quick shampoo, she motioned for me to go sit in her salon chair while she was drinking coffee and boppin' to an 80's song, "Girls just want to have fun."

She walked over and turned me away from the mirror. I could feel her chopping off the right side of my hair by my ear.

Then the song, "Wild Thing" came on and she's singing and flinging' hair telling me, "You are gonna love it!" I think her name was Jack!
She turned me toward the mirror so I could see myself and I was in shock!

This is how it came out!"

(Comedian's illustration)
Today, this might actually be in style…

Oh my, how a hair cut gone wrong can be depressing. Have you ever hated the way your hair looked?

How about the person who has the nerve to ask, "What happened to your hair?" or the people who just stare?

I have often been told, "My friend cut and colored my hair," when a client comes in for a corrective service. I ask, "Are they still you're friend?"

Have you ever felt like not coming out of your bathroom, let alone your home? I'll share with you how to make sure you are never a Victim again!

You won't have to spend hours trying to make a bad haircut look good. There are too many things to get done, too many people to see and too many people to be.

How about shopping? I love to shop! I used to shop whenever I needed to treat myself or if I was kind of down. I was once told I needed counseling for my shopping habits. I told them they must be crazy. Shopping *is* my therapy. Now I'm *their* personal shopper too.

I love vacations. You know, that's the time you want your hair to look great everyday so you get a *beachy* wave perm as the sign read, "Body Waves on Special." Great! ... Only to return home with a Bozo Perm or the Velcro Doo that sticks to the roof of your car! Your friends begin to wonder if you've been struck by lightning! Was the person who did your hair on drugs? Could be! The sign should have said," Permanent Blowout!"

Chapter 3
Finding an Artistic Hair Designer

It's important to find someone that is patient with you and interested in listening in order to help you explain what you want your hair to look like. When you find an artistic Hair Designer, show pictures and share any concerns or fears you may have.

Let them know you want your hair length left long if you do. Short styles are fun too, especially for those who love them. By taking the time to find a professional, artistic Hair Designer you will *always* look forward to having your hair cut and styled.

In this fashion conscious society a very practical part of our life begins each and every day when we look in the mirror.

When you look at yourself, are you happy with your hair? Would you like a change?

Perhaps some hair color would help restore youthful contrast with your complexion. You may love your hairdresser and you feel so dedicated to him or her that you wouldn't think of ever changing. You are very fortunate and blessed, considering you love your hair just as much.

Tens of thousands of Hair Dressers gather at the yearly hair shows hosted by the most prestigious distributors of hair care lines and beauty supply stores.

They are held in various convention halls and hotels in major cities around the world. Big hair shows are great, featuring hairstyles being demonstrated ranging from glamorous to outrageous.

The innovative and creative imaginations of some of the best Hair Designers come out to perform and play. With high energy flowing at its peak to inspire, teach and sell in creative fashion, models strut their new look from head to toe with ultimate confidence. Some of the costumes are avant-garde, some a bit dominatrix and some can be quite risqué.

There are competitions showcasing top talent from Beauty School students competing in fantasy looks. There are many choices with so much to see and learn with the newest tools of the trade in high tech.

An interesting fact about hair shows from around the globe is that most of the hairstyles shown in the past would rarely be worn out on the street.

Fast-forward to the present and anything goes. The more colorful and unique the design, the more attention the person wearing it is happy to receive.

Inspiration or perspiration depends on how you perceive it. A stylist with thirty or even fifty years of experience may have done it all and still ahead of their time. Some hairdressers with thirty years experience may be doing the exact same styles they learned thirty years ago. Keeping up to date is important.

Picture the anxious Hairstylist leaving the show with really big ideas, eagerly anticipating the next new client walking through the salon door; new hair cut styles running rampant through their mind after watching and wanting to practice the new techniques seen at the show with scissors, razor and triple shears. Finish up with the clippers on the sides, and… Viola!!! The widow spider cut comes to life! An incredible work of art. Too cool! Totally rad!

Everyone in the salon agrees except for the lady who's wearing it and her husband who can hardly recognize her! But hey dude, it's *killer*!

It's great for some people who want an outrageous hairstyle, but in the hands of an inexperienced hairstylist, this can be dangerous.

I am not saying that all hairdressers just out of school are inexperienced and unprofessional. A lot of them are natural, incredible artists that have found their calling. Then again, there are those who should be working in meat markets and I don't mean nightclubs.

There are some hair cutters who claim to know all the tricks of how to make a bad hair cut look good. No problem, a little mousse here, a little gel there, mega-spritz and spray, it looks good that day until the client tries to style it themselves at home.

Which reminds me of the time I went to have lunch with a hairdresser friend, Michael in Buffalo. When I arrived at his salon he had just hung up the phone.

He exclaimed, "Ahhh... I can't believe it... one of my clients just called me, I cut his hair the other day and he needs me to re-cut it. I have to wait a few minutes for him. He's coming right in, would you mind waiting?" I told him I didn't mind at all.

We talked for a bit about the hair biz and soon the client Michael spoke of walked in the salon.

I observed Michael being himself, Italian and a native New Yorker with a personality that entertained.

The scene I witnessed between Michael and his client went like this:

Michael combed through his clients hair and ran his fingers through it with a puzzled look on his face like something was stinky.

His client said, "Look, it sticks up and out over there and it won't go back over here."

Michael was silent as he combed his client's hair a few more times looking intently at his client's head. He stood back, crossed his arms with concern and said, "It must be the way you slept last night. Waddaya want me to do about it?"

The client got a disturbed look on his face and said, "Well I think it's cut crooked, it's longer behind my ear on this side than on the other!"

Michael studied his hair from *every* angle again, held his comb up like he was measuring the difference and said, "Ahh, I know what happened! It's because of the way you were sitting in my chair when I cut your hair. You must have crossed your legs while you were leaning to the left, reading that People magazine. "I'll fix it for ya, fogeddabout it."

Michael looked over at me rolling his eyes up to the ceiling as if to say, "This guy is nuts!"
Truth be told, his client's hair was quite a mess.
I learned a lot that day about what some clients have to go through to get a decent hair cut.

You may be the client who goes home to restyle your hair right after you have it professionally styled because you feel that no one can make you look as good as you can. Sound familiar?

For most, it's probably true....

You may be the client who loves the way your stylist makes your hair look and cannot seem to do it the same way at home. In this case, I suggest asking your stylist for a lesson. I show my clients when they let me know or ask.

What if your Hair Designer has no time to give you a styling lesson? What's one to do? Change?
Now that's a tough one. Ask them who might be able to help you or if you could make an

appointment for a shampoo/blow-dry service with a styling lesson. The appointment should take about forty-five minutes. You will learn new techniques with a brush and a blow dryer.

A professional Hair Designer is like a surgeon, with the knowledge of a chemist, mathematician and an artist, able to design a hairstyle suited to you.

Where do you find this so called artistic professional Hair Designer?

You will not find one for a ten-dollar hair cut at a budget salon… unless you happen to find a diamond in the rough.

Another important factor in finding the right Hair Designer for you is to find one that you can trust.

A Hair Designer should be a confidant and you should be able to trust them with your hair *and* your words.

Hair Designers, Hairdressers, Hairstylists and Beauty Operators come from different walks of life and some even walk different.

A hairdresser is a universal term referring to someone whose occupation is to cut or style hair in order to change or maintain a person's image.

A hairdresser is synonymous with a hairstylist and will typically work in a hair salon or on location at fashion events, movie sets, weddings, etc. A hairdresser dresses the hair. They can take the *same cut* and make *different styles* out of it.

From casual to formal with a few pins and hair spray, a Hair Designer that has advanced training and experience will be able to create an unlimited number of hair styles and able to look at any picture and duplicate the style as long as the client has similar hair texture and facial shape.

The weekly shampoo sets of teasing with lots of hairspray are still alive and thriving in some salons. If you *would* like a change on the cutting edge of fashion, an artistic Hair Designer is skilled in refreshing your present look with an up-to-date haircut and style.

Whatever you are looking for, find it by asking questions. There are professionals and nonprofessionals, experienced and inexperienced practitioners and then there are true artists.

A Hair Designer is professionally trained to plan or design the chosen hairstyle by executing the desired hair cut according to a predetermined plan.

Taking all the facets of your individual hair type, facial shape and body structure into consideration are a must.

A professional Hair Designer is experienced in creating volume and height with cutting techniques and/or by applying products to give the hair more body. Sometimes a full or partial body wave is the best choice if the hair is in good condition.

Today there are new products available that don't contain chemicals in order to keep your hair in the best condition.

You will know you have found the right Hair Designer when you're thoughts and ideas coincide with theirs by effectively communicating with each other so that your desired outcome can be fully achieved.

Sometimes it takes months to have the look you desire. It may take growing your hair out in certain areas to create the desired style.

Finding a Hair Designer who is willing to help you achieve your goal is worth his or her weight in gold. You will look the way you have always wanted to look.

On the other hand, (I think it's the left) you may have a Hair Designer who *insists* on doing what *they* want with an attitude.

By claiming that their haircuts are like their *signature* and you should just trust them regardless of what you have told them you want.

Well now what do we have here? An ego problem, or perhaps a new series called, Fatal Distraction?

How do you find the right Hair Designer for you? How do you find the best of everything? These days you might find one on Yelp, Facebook or Google!

Perhaps the best way to find one is by word of mouth. Here's the funny thing about that: when someone receives a really bad haircut they will tell twenty people or anyone who will listen.

Even when they are waiting in line at the store, they will turn to any stranger... anyone who will listen to their whole story about how they were victimized. When someone receives a great haircut, they usually don't say anything unless they are complimented. I guess one could be a little modest when their hair look's so incredible!

When you see someone with a great haircut and you want to know where he or she went to get it done, try complimenting them.

Don't feel awkward, go ahead, and ask them who did their hair. You might just get the referral of a Hair Designer you've always wanted.

Don't be afraid to ask around. You may be new in town or maybe you've lived in the same city all your life and still can't find a good one. If this is the case, come to California and see me. Call for an appointment first please.

Places like shopping malls are great for fashion.

Why not shop around for hairstyles you see on the people walking by?

Not like a stalker… don't start circling the person. Just be casual about it. Stop in stores and check out the sales girl's hairstyles and ask them where they went to get such a great style. They will be flattered and you just might hit the jackpot!

Stop into a salon and explain as you are looking at their retail products that you are looking for a new salon and ask if you can sit in the reception area to observe the stylists. If they say no you wouldn't want to go there anyway.

Here's another idea: look up a neighborhood salon online and call to ask if you can get a conditioning treatment. Make an appointment for a conditioning treatment or for a manicure so you can watch all the hairdressers in action.

This goes for men and women. If you see a hairdresser that has the haircut or style you like, ask them who does their hair. Then go to the person in the salon that gave them such a great style.

You will be able to tell how good the stylists are in a salon by how great *their* hair looks. If they are dressed like they just cleaned their house with no make-up on etc., beware. If you walk in and notice really awful or damaged looking hairstyles at a place you have made an appointment at just say, "Sorry I can't keep my appointment, something urgent has just come up" (like a whole lot of discernment on your part to run away as fast as you can)

Be sure you set up a consultation *before* anyone touches your hair or any service is rendered. It will give you a chance to ask the Hair Designer how long they have been doing hair.

Hopefully you have looked at their portfolio of work on their salon website to see some examples of their work. It's important for you to feel confident with the person doing your hair.

When you go to a Doctor for the first time, you have to fill out a form describing what you're feeling. They need to know all kinds of information about you. Would you have a doctor try to figure out what you need by just looking at you?

It seems quite natural to sit in the Hair Designer's chair, telling him or her, "Do what ever you think." But think about this for a minute… we pay a dentist to look in our mouth, but they have to take an x-ray to be sure of what is needed.

I know someone who worked as a dental assistant who told me she quit her job because the Dentist she worked for pulled the wrong tooth from a lady's mouth and didn't tell her.

He then pulled the *right* tooth and made up a story telling her he had a bridge he wanted to sell her.

My mother always told me, it takes all kinds.
But she never said how many!

The world we live in is full of new technology in everything we do. Everybody wants to stay young, healthy and beautiful. It's smart to spend your money on health and beauty where it pays off in the long run.

Chapter 4
A Winning Consultation

It's important to tell your Hair Designer about the hair services you have received or applied yourself to your hair in the last six months to a year.

Doing this will increase your chances of being completely understood and getting what you hope for. Hair that has been cosmetically treated with certain products can prevent any new service from being successful.

In my experience there have been times when clients have not been completely honest about coloring their own hair or putting too many inferior products on their hair. There is nothing worse than being a victim from the very beginning. The Hair Designer could be the victim in this case. It's imperative to be honest about previous chemical services.

It can be difficult for a Hair Designer to tell what chemical services have been applied to the client's hair just by looking at it. I can tell to a large degree what I can or cannot do to fulfill a client's request. Although I have been trained in the study of hair under the microscope, not every Hair Designer has this experience.

> *"Love of beauty is taste…*
> *The creation of beauty is art."*
> *- Ralph Waldo Emerson*

A beautiful young woman walked in my salon requesting a hair color that would look awful with her skin tone. I chose to decline from coloring her hair and explained why it would not be her best choice. I urged her to go to a wig shop and try on a wig that same color in the picture she showed me. At first she felt I should be able to give her what she wanted.

I asked her to trust me and then she left a bit confused. I wasn't quite sure if I would ever hear from her again.

I was concerned, so two days later I called her and asked if she went to try on the wig with the color she wanted.

She said, "Oh yes, my mother went with me and you were right, the color looked terrible with my skin tone, but why can't I have highlights without brassiness? I only wanted to bleach all my hair out like Christine Aguilera's because I don't want the brass." I told her I could highlight her hair without brass and I did. She was very happy.

I've had many clients with stories I will never forget like the one about a hairdresser I knew named Nick who owned a salon called, "His n' Hers". He didn't know how to do perms and he needed help with a new client.

It was for a woman about sixty years old. She walked in the salon smoking and grunting and sat down in the reception area. Her name was Norma. I asked her to sit in my chair and she was very quiet.

I smiled and said, "Hi, I'm Tricia. I understand you would like a body perm today?"

She just stared into the mirror at herself with beady eyes and said in a loud gruff voice, "Do something with it!"

I looked over at Nick as he raised his eyebrows and walked over to give me his opinion.

I was speechless as I tried to remove the hairpins in her hair because they were stuck like glue. Nick also tried to pull them out and failed.

"Well," he said, "I have some WD-40 around here somewhere."

Actually, he had to go buy some. I waited patiently as I watched this Lady smoke and grunt incessantly.

I found out later from Nick that this poor woman had come by taxi from a nearby Hospital where she had been in a ward for three months surviving a nervous breakdown. Nick finally returned and sprayed her hair with the WD-40. It was like magic how the pins came out so easily.

I put on some rubber gloves and shampooed her hair about seven times. She grunted the whole time!

Nick found it quite comical with a smirk on his face while watching the whole scene.

Her hair turned out great and she was very happy as she grunted out the door.

I would like to add that it's important for clients to understand that going to the salon when you are sick with a cold or flu is disrespectful to the Hair Designer or anyone else in the salon.

On the other side of the coin, neither should the Hair Designer come to work when they are sick. Personally, I feel disrespected when a client comes into my salon and exposes me to germs that should be kept at home.

You are in very close proximity with your Hair Designer. Having respect for each other is crucial in maintaining a good relationship. Try to be courteous concerning fresh breath, cleanliness and health. Our first impression is the most important anywhere we go.

When you arrive at the salon for your appointment you should feel good about the atmosphere. The receptionist should be polite if there is one. When greeted by the Hair Designer, hopefully he or she greets you with a handshake and a smile.

Be sure to notice the floor. Is it clean? You don't want to be sitting in a chair with someone else's hair around it.

Let them know that you are there for a consultation and ask your new Hair Designer for guidance on how to make you look your absolute best.

I tell my clients that the reason some people never look like they age is that they've found a hairstyle that makes them look their best and they keep it.

I understand that a lot of clients want change and enjoy many styles. Especially as one gets older, finding the best look and keeping it does wonders for appearing ageless.

When people ask me, "How old are you? I respond with two words, "I'm ageless" with a smile.

At your consultation, some questions you might be asked are:

1. What is the preferred length for your hair?

2. Do you remember a time you loved your hair the most?

3. How much time do you have to style your hair at home?

4. What's your occupation?

5. Are you interested in hair color to complement your haircut?

6. What type of products do you use on your hair?

From your answers the Hair Designer should have a pretty good idea for determining what would be best for your hair and what it will or won't do in terms of style.

There are many options to enhance and support your desired style and this is the time to discuss hair color, highlighting, smoothing or straightening services, body waves or perms.

During many consultations with clients rather than just looking in the mirror, I have found eye-to-eye contact while communicating with each other before any service is rendered very important. This will result in a higher level of confidence in your new Hair Designer.

Be sure to discuss what you would like at each hair appointment. There are occasions when a stylist will get so busy working on multiple clients with an assistant helping to shampoo and blow dry hair that a mix-up might accidentally occur. You could walk out of the salon with someone else's haircut!

I love my clients. I have a great time getting to know them and watching them walk out the door invigorated and beautified.

When meeting with a new Hair Designer, A word to the wise: try to be very careful not to bad-mouth your last hairdresser as it will give your present one a potential high sign, that perhaps *you* might be the problem.

If it turns out that your hair was unevenly cut, I'm sure your Hair Designer will be able to see it when cutting and correct it. Please make sure you allow enough time for the services necessary when you make your appointment. Be careful not to rush a haircut or color or even a perm. Having to pick someone up or be at another appointment could be uncomfortable for you both. Schedule accordingly.

Hair straightening treatments and corrective hair color services can take up to four hours or more depending on your hair length. It's always a good idea to eat before you go or bring a snack with you. Relax and enjoy your time while you get beautified.

Bringing pictures in is a great idea. I really like it when a client brings in pictures as I enjoy creating new looks and modifying a style to go with their facial features and hair texture.

At this point I must caution you. In my experience there are times when the latest, most popular style is on everyone's head. Trying to look like the latest fashion model or TV actor that has a hairdresser by their side for every camera shoot or show, may tell the stylist you are caught up in an illusion.

If you are happy with your present hairstyle and hair length, be sure to ask the Hair Designer to follow the lines of your current haircut. Tell him or her to take off a half-an-inch or more using discretion all over by just trimming it and don't ever be shy about asking them not to get "scissor happy."

I say this only because I have watched it happen in the chair next to me. Some hairdressers will only trim off what you ask. Others will trim what you ask and then check the cut by what is called cross checking, cutting more hair off again and again. Before you know it, you're hair is about two and a half inches shorter and the hairdresser dries your hair exclaiming out loud... "Gee... ah...
You're hair sure shrinks a lot when you dry it, HUH?

I'll let you in on a little secret: hair cutting combs are marked with a ruler measuring seven inches long. Ask to see the comb and measure out exactly what you want cut off.

I know this might sound a little OCD, but it may be the difference between becoming a victim or not. Don't be self-conscious about asking how much the salon services cost and how often you will need to come in to maintain your hairstyle.

I call it maintenance because if your hair appointments are kept up on a regular basis, you will always look great. Look at how many times a year you may need your hair done and mark it on your calendar. When you think about it that way, considering the fact your hair will look good all year long, the cost will be well worth it. When a special occasion comes up, you don't have to stress out. Superior quality is priceless.

Having an artistic Hair Designer cut and style your hair helps to hold the shape longer. A cheap hair cut will have you going back more often because when your hair starts sticking out on one side and lying flat on the top, the only thing you can think of doing is to get it cut again. You will most likely think to yourself... "I guess it's just my hair, I must have bad hair!"

If you ever feel uncomfortable with how you've been treated during a consultation or a hair appointment, you have the right to just get up and leave! After all, it's your hair and your money.

Before they begin cutting your hair you can just excuse yourself, there's no contract to hold you against your will.

Perhaps a familiar experience comes to mind from the past when having your hair completely ruined changed your sweet, kind nature.

Don't feel alone. Almost everyone has undergone a similar experience. Remember, it's not what happens to you, but how you deal with it that's most important.

Keep this in mind as well... A skilled artist pays attention to detail. Artistic Hair Designers truly care and are passionate about their work. Once upon a time *I* was the victim. I felt like Goldilocks in the clutches of my big bad boss. Let me explain:

My hair is thick, coarse and naturally curly. Underneath at the nape (back) of my neck, it is only slightly wavy, so the owner of the salon where I was working decided she wanted to perm that area to make my hair fuller in the back.

Hmm-good idea, or so I thought.

She permed the back section of my hair leaving the solution on too long and it burned my hair to a crispy frizz.

In my defense, I had asked her to check it after five minutes but she insisted my hair needed more time.

I just sat there numb and impatient until this very strong odorous fragrance was finally rinsed off my hair. I knew she was wrong about the timing, but what could I do? SHE was THE BOSS...

It took almost two years to grow out new healthy hair. There I was, looking at my hair in the mirror asking myself, "What am I going to do?" Fighting tears...

After that episode I moved to another salon. It's no fun being a victim of my own profession, however if sharing this experience will help YOU... then I WIN! (And so do you). That's what this book is all about.

Sometimes there is nothing you can do but wait it out. You could buy a hat or shave your head and join a rock band. You could beat on some congas or something to help you get over any anger you may have or you can forgive the person and let it go.

*"Forgiveness is the fragrance
the violet sheds on the heel
that has crushed it."*
- Mark Twain

Chapter 5
Let's Talk About Style

The term "In style" refers to the latest look or fad, be it in the winter, spring, summer or fall. Do you have your own unique way of wearing your hair? Are your clothes and accessories in style whatever the season? How about inner style? Do you feel good about yourself no matter what you are wearing?

The hairstyle that will look the best on *you* depends on many factors. A hairstyle that is balanced with your body frame creates a "total look". A great haircut will enhance your facial features, your neck and shoulders.

Hair color should complement your skin tone and eye color. All of these factors have to be taken into consideration for the best overall style.

Having long hair or short hair depends on what looks best on you and what length makes you feel beautiful. I have heard clients say they cannot grow their hair past their shoulders.

I have suggested they loosely secure their hair up in a cloth covered "scrunchy" on the top of their head at night when they sleep. This way the pillow and the sheets do not cause the hair to weaken and break off. It works and I have clients in their sixties who finally have hair past their shoulders and love it.

Framing your face is key, as your face is divided into three areas. From the forehead to eyebrows is one third. From the eyebrows to end of your nose is the next third and from the end of your nose to the bottom of your chin the final third.

A good way to find out is to put your hair up in a towel and stand in front of the mirror. By using a measuring tape, try measuring the distance at the three divisions I mentioned earlier.

Facial shapes can be easily determined and you should know what your facial shape is. There are seven different types. Do you know which one you have? Here are the seven facial shapes:

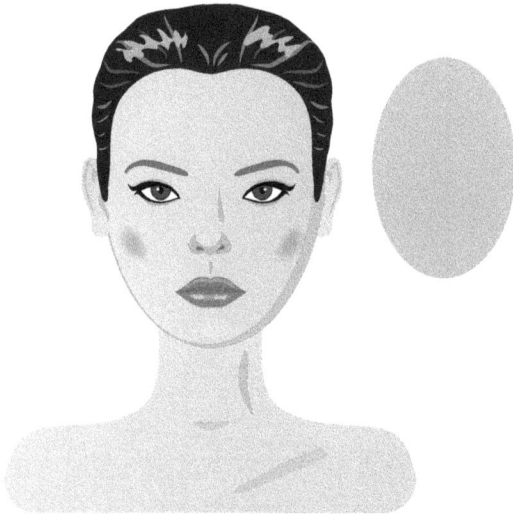

OVAL

The oval shaped face, as you may already know is considered the perfect facial shape. You can wear any style. Your face is one and a half times longer than the width at the brow. Your forehead is slightly wider than your chin.

ROUND

The round shaped face is round at the hairline and the chin-line. You want to create the illusion of length to the face by styling the hair with height on top, bangs to one side with hair covering the ears and part of the cheeks.

SQUARE

The square shaped face has a straight hairline across the forehead. You want to add length to offset the square. Your style should lift off the forehead with a diagonal part adding some fullness and wave with hair coming forward at the sides of your face and jaw-line to create the illusion of narrowing your face.

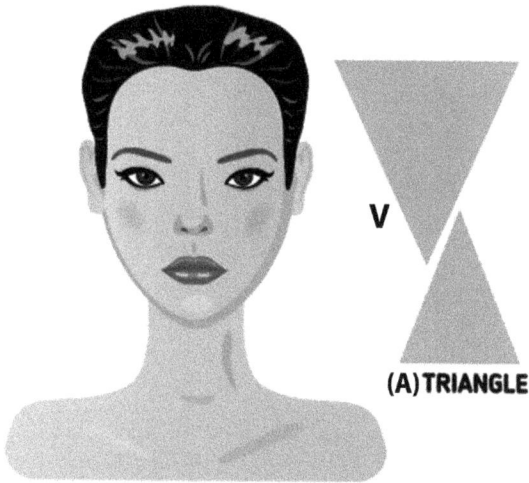

(A)TRIANGLE

(V)TRIANGLE

For the A triangle or pear shaped face with a wide
chin and narrow forehead the hair should be worn
with no bangs and fullness at jawline or longer.
The V triangle or pear shaped face has a narrow
chin and jaw-line and a wide forehead needing a lot
of height and fullness at the top (a partial perm or
body wave is recommended) for the illusion of
width around your forehead, with wispy bangs and
some layered curls at your jaw-line to soften the
chin-line creating more of an oval appearance.

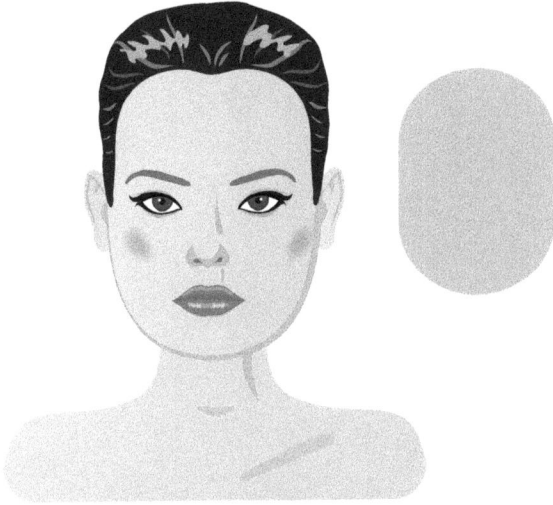

OBLONG

The oblong shaped face is long and narrow with
hollow cheeks. You want to make your face appear
shorter and wider. Your hair should be styled full at
the sides away from your face with waves and curls
at any length. Unless your eyes are close-set, you
will want your hair swept up with bangs on one side
falling over the eyebrow to help reduce the length
of your face.

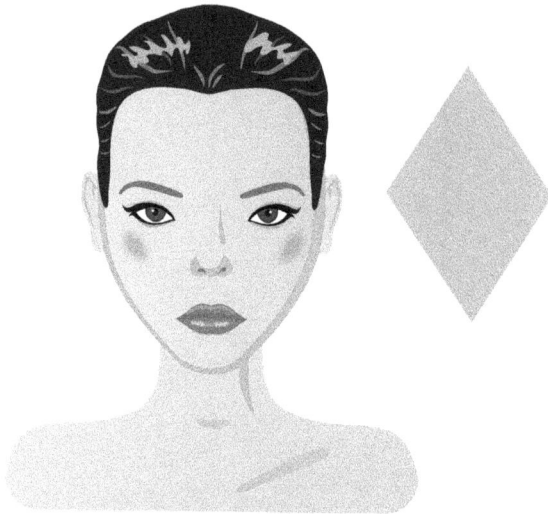

DIAMOND

The diamond shaped face has a narrow chin and forehead and wide through the cheekbones. You want to decrease the appearance of width across the cheekbone area by increasing fullness at the forehead and jaw-line. Styling layered hair close to the face at the cheekbones helps to create the illusion of an oval shape.

HEART

The heart shaped face has a narrow chin-line and wide forehead. You want to reduce the width of your forehead by styling your hair with a center part unless you have wide-set eyes, in which case a style swept over to one side is more attractive. Hair should be at least chin length or longer.

Whatever the shape of your face, there are great styles to make you look your best. Try taking a picture of yourself with your hair back and away from your face and use it to create the perfect look for you. The key is to imagine an oval shape and anything outside of the oval can be drawn in with hair, then cut and styled to improve your look.

Tracing paper can be bought at any art store or drug store. Put the tracing paper over your photograph and draw hair around your face. You can do this on your own and bring it in to your stylist. You just might be surprised with the outcome.

I think those computers that alter your hair into a new style on a video screen are interesting. For a while they were displayed in shopping malls. There are a few salons that still use them, but I noticed that the computer images tended to slightly alter your face as well as the style.

One of my clients received a gift certificate to have computer images taken with the most suited hairstyles for her facial shape. She brought them into the salon to show me and her face looked much thinner in her four computer photographs than in person. The styles were ok but only one really looked good for her. I guess that's better than none. All the others changed how she looked considerably.

Occasionally I'll draw my clients face on paper and sketch a hairstyle for their review before I ever touch their hair with scissors.

Sometimes clients will come in for a consultation and can't decide what they want. I believe it's up to the Hair Designer to help them figure it out. It may be that two or three different hairstyles have to be blended together to create the look they want to achieve.

Generally speaking, most people know what they want but clearly defining it to a Hair Designer might be difficult. Finding someone who will listen to you is more than half the battle.

We are living in the communication age and there are times when people's lives are in difficult circumstances. Some will think a new hairstyle will help to change how they feel. After all, your hair is something you can constantly change.

I had a client named Suzy. I could see that she was emotionally upset. She had beautiful thick blond hair almost to her waist. In the beginning of our consultation, she asked me to cut all her hair off into a short bob. I mean really short! I looked at her like she was crazy and told her there was no way I would do that. Struggling to hold back her tears... she asked, "Why not?"

I gently told her my intuition was telling me this was an impulsive decision and if she felt the same way tomorrow, I would be glad to cut it really short. She responded by telling me about an argument she had with her husband. She wanted to cut off all her hair to get back at him. I talked with her for a while and calmed her down before she went home. She called me the next day and told me she made up with her husband and thanked me a hundred times for not cutting her hair short.

I feel it's important to care about each client by keeping notes on prior services and details on how they wish their hair to be cut, colored and styled.

I find it helps in building a healthy bond between the client and the Hair Designer.

Now, if I had cut Suzy's hair short, who knows what would have come of it? Which reminds me of one of the main reasons I decided to write, "Frazzle to Dazzle."

I moved to California after having finished Beauty school in N.Y. While attending school full time to complete the extra six hundred hours for the cosmetology exam in California I worked as a cocktail server at a very nice dinner house called the Velvet Turtle.

One evening while I was working, I was in the lounge talking with some customers when all of a sudden we heard the sound of a gunshot. Out in the parking lot about forty feet away from the restaurant a woman had gotten into her car and shot herself. (God rest her soul) I didn't know her but I heard the story from the hairdresser who did the poor woman's hair.

She explained to me that this client was depressed and having a lot of trouble in her marriage.

The client left the salon crying, she was disappointed with her haircut and style and suddenly decided to take her own life.

I felt compassion for this hairdresser. What a huge responsibility it is I thought... to be in this business. The whole situation had truly affected me.

Quite often this hairdresser was coming into the restaurant to talk to me. I got to know her pretty well and she invited me to her home for a Christmas party. Looking around at her home, I could tell she had been very successful in the beauty business.

The following year would be her last year in the profession. This trauma had truly changed her feelings about her work. The whole experience left me with a lot to consider as well.

When licensed to work on people or dealing with the public on such a personal level, there are natural consequences to be expected.

This tragedy was not the hairdresser's fault. She was a victim of circumstance. Only God knows what was going on in her client's mind.

I sincerely give a hundred percent to each and every person who sits in my chair. I honestly listen and want each person to feel great about how they look with a beautifying transformation that includes being emotionally lifted up ...as they walk out the salon door.

Although no one is perfect, I feel I've had a really good track record.

I would say that some of the most gratifying moments I have experienced working in my salon have been from receiving the approval of my skills and talent from clients and friends after giving them a beautiful cut, color and style.

In my salon I strive to create a harmonious environment where one can let their hair down.

I do understand some clients just use hairdressers to do their hair and just want the "factory usual".

And then, there are some people you just can't please...

One of the dilemmas in this business is how Hair Designers can be taken advantage of. For instance, a client may walk in and request a perm, color or a highlight when the condition of their hair implies disaster. I have refused to comply, no matter how much money I could have earned that day.

I would recommend conditioning treatments for the client to get their hair in good condition and then secure them a future appointment for the actual desired hair service.

Unfortunately some clients will not take "no" for an answer, insisting that if they are willing to pay for a hair service, they should be able to get what they want.

I tell you, I would rather the client go down the street to someone else at another salon. I value my reputation and protect it by refusing service in such cases. It's always better to do that than to damage their hair any further.

The last thing I want to be is a co-dependent Hair Designer or a "bad-hair enabler".

(But they *are* out there)
I have learned to listen to my intuition and not the client begging me to do *whatever.* Co-dependent no more!

My reputation is much more important than the thought of losing a client. Taking a chance on a client's hair that is damaged from previous chemical services is never a good idea.

Honesty is the best policy! I find nine times out of ten the client is thankful for my concern. Besides, how can anyone in the beauty business ever think they will get away with causing someone the embarrassment of having ruined their hair?

People who live in the limelight have to look great all the time and they cannot afford mistakes. The Hair Designers to the stars are skillfully trained artistic experts.

Have you ever wondered why some movie stars never change their hairstyle? Some fashion models' hairstyles are famous. Remember Farrah Fawcett? Her hairstyle was quite famous. Her Hair Designer, Allen Edwards designed her famous shag haircut.

The word shag did not just become popular with Austin Powers.

As a matter of fact, shags are really cool *now* and back in style. It's one of my favorite styles to cut. Allen Edwards is currently designing innovative cuts and thriving in Los Angeles… I met Allen with his beautiful wife at a gathering held by a dear friend of ours.

Has anyone ever told you that you never seem to age? In most cases the person receiving this compliment hasn't changed their hairstyle through the years and has a healthy diet and good character.

They may have slight variations on the same style, a little longer here, shorter there, etc., but basically the same style.

They have found their perfect cut, making them look their absolute best. Their hairstyle is actually helping to keep them younger looking as the year's go on.

Clients come in and show me movie star hairstyles and want their hair cut the same way. I do my best to make it happen for them and so should your Hair Designer.

"We delight in the beauty of the butterfly,
but rarely admit the changes it has gone through
to achieve that beauty."
-   Maya Angelou

Essentially hairstyles come and go and some return, a classic style looks great no matter what the year, season or dress and is a stamp of personal style when it comes to fashion.

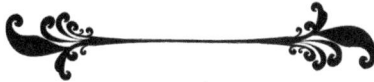

"Knowing your angles logically with
good timing is the precision and
shape of you and what you do
[hair and life]."
-ABB

Chapter 6
Hair Lingo

To be a master in the art of cutting and styling requires a definite learning period and countless hours of practice. One of the biggest problems encountered in hair services is the wrong use of terminology and cutting techniques.

I have seen this kind of communication breakdown again and again. I'll never forget the time I worked at a prestigious department store salon. The chain was international and well known. I learned some interesting things there. I had been a Hair Designer for about seven years. When I moved to a different state, I had to start all over again and I found one of the best ways to build a clientele was to go to a classy department store salon. Department stores advertise when they hire new employees. Clients get a hair cut deal at a fraction of the cost with no appointment needed; just walk in.

Picture this scene if you will; There are about twenty hairdressers working together in this fairly large salon and you can pretty much see and hear everything that goes on.

Right next to me is a young girl who just graduated from beauty school. A male client about forty years old is sitting in her chair. He explained to her that he is very particular about his hair. He expressed the importance of having his hair cut over his ears. The young girl nervously says, "Oh sure, sounds great."

She begins cutting his hair on the left side by his ear. The guy is watching her every snip through the mirror.

All of a sudden he yells, "Stop!"

She looks at him surprised and asked, "What's wrong?" He said, "I specifically asked you to cut my hair *over* my ear, not *above* my ear!"

She was stunned. I looked over and saw he was really disgusted. He said, "Go ahead and cut the other side short to match."

She was on the verge of tears looking over at me and there was nothing she could do. The poor guy exclaimed he now had to wait about two months for his hair to grow long enough to cover the large ears he was trying to camouflage.

Please understand that hair cutting in essence is art, geometry and mathematics. Your head profile is like the shape of a protractor.

A Hair Designer's tools are in their mind and hands. There are precise consequences to every cut that is executed.

A skilled, artistic Hair Designer knows the theory and practical knowledge to always be successful at cutting hair. Executing plan A is best, better than resorting to plan B if you get what I mean.

Haircutting Terms

I feel it's important for you to be informed and you will discover more terms in chapter nine.

For now these are some hair cutting terms you might want to be familiar with to effectively communicate with your Hair Designer.

Bang (fringe)
Front section of the hair that is above the forehead (middle) and ends at the corners of the outer part of your eyebrows.

Beveling
A technique using diagonal lines by cutting hair ends with a slight increase or decrease in length helping the ends to go under – If this is desired, ask for a beveled cut.

Blunt haircut
A haircut where all the hair is one length with no layers, one length that forms a weight line. The hair is cut with no elevation or over-direction.

More Terms

Growth pattern
The direction in which the hair grows from the scalp also referred to as natural fall or natural falling position.

Layered haircut
A gradated effect achieved by cutting the hair with elevation or over-direction; the hair is cut at higher elevations, creating layer movement and volume in the hair.

A great hair cut is more than just reducing length and bulk from the hair. It begins with careful assessment, and application of quality tools in skilled hands.

A dynamic haircut may include techniques with shears, razors, clippers, thinning shears, and all the conventional tools such as combs and brushes.

Chapter 7
Hair Color & Body Waves
Smoothing & Straightening

Hair coloring is one of the most fun and rewarding services offered at a salon. Many stylists shy away from color because of the possible problems and mistakes that could happen. I'll share with you some knowledge and techniques to help you understand what's going on during your professional hair color service.

One of my clients asked me how long a hair color formula should stay on the hair and what happens if you leave it on too long.

I told her it depends on the service and hair color product. If I were coloring the roots for a retouch and the formulas processing time calls for 25 or 30 minutes and it is left on a few minutes longer, it's ok because the developer stops working after so many minutes.

The hair color developers consist of different volumes of hydrogen peroxide and your Hair Designer should know how long it is active when mixed with hair color.

For clients with darker hair wanting to have blonde highlights, hydrogen peroxide is mixed with bleach. Now, this is a different story because the bleach formula keeps on working to lighten the hair when higher volumes are used.

When bleach is mixed with a high volume developer can damage the hair if left on past the lightest blonde stage.

If the bleached hair turns white from being left on too long it could turn almost transparent giving you mushy hair. It could break off at the ends and make you very unhappy. If more bleach than hydrogen peroxide is mixed and the manufacturers instructions are not being followed, the hair could be so damaged it could break off at the scalp.

A more experienced Hair Designer will have the chemistry knowledge to avoid these potential disasters.

A client's hair that is darker than a level five or a (medium brown) needs a higher volume developer to achieve a blonde hair color. High lift hair colors can lift four to five levels without bleach. Ask your Hair Designer to show you your natural color with a hair color swatch chart. You don't want your highlights more than 4 levels lighter or your hair will look striped like a zebra.

I want to help you to understand that unless you have virgin hair, bleaching over hair that has been colored a few times may dry it out. You will need to get some treatments that are not sold in your supermarket or drug store. Ask your Hair Designer about ampoules of protein to restructure your hair.

I want to let you know that many store-bought hair color products contain metallic salts that stain the cuticle layer of the hair. The cuticle layer of the hair should remain transparent and allow the color to shine through by reflecting light when professional hair color is used.

When you see people who continually color their hair with store-bought products, the hair looks dull like shoe polish and doesn't shine. It's like taking stain for wood and painting it on the hair.

Hair color products are classified into the following subtypes according to color permanence: temporary, semi-permanent, demi-permanent and permanent.

My favorite hair color product line to work with is called Framesi, a product from Milan, Italy. In its simplicity, it offers the most predictable hair color. What I like about it is how the hair colors look as natural as a child's hair in every shade and tone.

Having read what we've covered so far, it's likely that you will now notice hair color, texture and hair health on others. If you see someone with a "natural" (not pink, blue or multi-striped) hair color that appears to be "dull" or non-reflective under natural light, they most likely have colored their own hair or suffered a hair color service from an inexperienced hairdresser.

Here is just a little theory on hair color…

Hair color may be warm or cool, based on the amount of red, yellow or blue contained in each chosen color.

Through the years as a corrective hair colorist I have corrected thousands of clients' hair color. I can pretty much tell you it's a combination of art and science including, chemistry, math and geometry to determine the right procedure.

Framesi hair color from Milan, Italy is very gentle on the hair and has a developer/activator with a vegetable coconut oil cream base.

Coconut oil is superior to all vegetable oils in penetrating the hair to minimize protein loss during a color service. It's good for cooking too! I mean the one in the supermarket, not the beauty store.

It also has superior gray coverage, adding a lot of shine to the hair with vitamin C, an anti-oxidant that fights against free radicals. It helps to stabilize color and prevent color fading while reserving a youthful vitality to your hair.

To help you understand gray hair better and why it turns out different than you might have expected, I have to explain...

The color you chose for the hair color swatch in the salon or on the photo of the model on the hair color box in the store may be what you desire, and it is possible. It's just that when the hair is gray or white it lacks pigment or color in the cortex. To replace it, a Hair Designer has to mix the right combination of the primary colors into the shade and tone of the formula; otherwise the hair turns brassy or that unattractive mousy color.

I would like to just lay out the foundation of application and the results that follow:

Virgin hair may be darkened or lightened with hair color products. Once your hair has been colored, making it any lighter requires using bleach or a color remover to lift out the hair color in order to lighten it.

You cannot lift color with color. For example, if you have natural gray hair and you colored your hair a medium to dark brown color and you want to be a lighter blonde, going to the store to get a lighter hair color to lift it up will not be successful.

If your hair has an ash tone, it has a high volume of red color molecules in it. If the right volume developer is not used, it will turn brassy. A good (experienced) hair colorist will know this.

To help you understand hair color levels, hair color is darkest at level one and lightest at level eleven or twelve depending on the hair color product line.

Bleach is mixed with a developer to be used as a hair lightener when you want it to be lighter in levels or very blonde followed by a toner.

A toner is a type of color generally applied after the hair has been pre-lightened with bleach.

For a natural, ash, honey, beige, or champagne tone, the client's skin tone is referenced to determine the best outcome.

Semi-permanent or demi-color is a temporary hair color that will darken your hair but it will not lighten it. Semi-permanent color lasts about six weeks and covers approximately 50% grey. Demi-color is a little stronger and lasts longer, about eight weeks and covers about 70% grey.

Hair Designers giving you highlights from either hair color or bleach can make a beautiful difference in your hairstyle. A partial or full highlight for your hair depends on the cut and style in mind.

To know what color highlights are best for you, consider the little specks of color in the iris of your eyes. These specks of color are the perfect color for your highlights.

If you have brown eyes and brunette hair or black hair, a few shades lighter in a chocolate, red or mahogany tone would be a great choice for highlights. After all, you want a highlight color to enhance not looked striped. Well, some do I guess. Be who you are and be happy.

Low-lights are darker than your current color and work best when using a deposit only color so they don't wash out. When blonde hair has gotten too light and some contrast is needed, lowlights are the answer.

Here's some inside information on hair:

The hair shaft is made up of three major components. From outermost layer to innermost, these consist of the cuticle, cortex, and the medulla.

The cuticle forms a protective barrier around the entire hair shaft. The cortex of the hair shaft contains bundles of keratin fibers, arranged in a vertical, rod-like fashion, that actually give shape and support to the hair structure.

All human hair has a cuticle and cortex, but very few have a medulla.

Q. What's a medulla? A. The innermost part of the hair strand.

The texture of hair determines if the hair is fine, medium or coarse. Hair texture can be described as smooth or rough.

There are three main types of hair:

Caucasian (European) hair can be straight, wavy or curly. It varies in color from dark brown to very light blonde.

African Caribbean hair is usually very tightly curled and usually dark in color.

Asian hair is often straight from very dark to medium brown and can be thick and very strong.

There are variables including the thickness, density and diameter of each strand of hair.

Regarding density, if the hair is too thin it may not hold the shape of a desired style correctly. If it is to thick it may not suit the chosen haircut as well unless modified by using texturizing shears.

Density relates to the number of hairs on the head. The number of hairs on the head depends on many factors and could vary but average densities are believed to be:
For natural blonde hair - 130,000
For red hair - 80,000

For brown hair - 100,000

For black hair - 100,000

On our heads, we have hundreds of thousands of follicles; each follicle produces many hairs throughout our lifetime.

Hair Follicle

As new hair grows the older hair is pushed out.

Structure and arrangement of the hair follicle

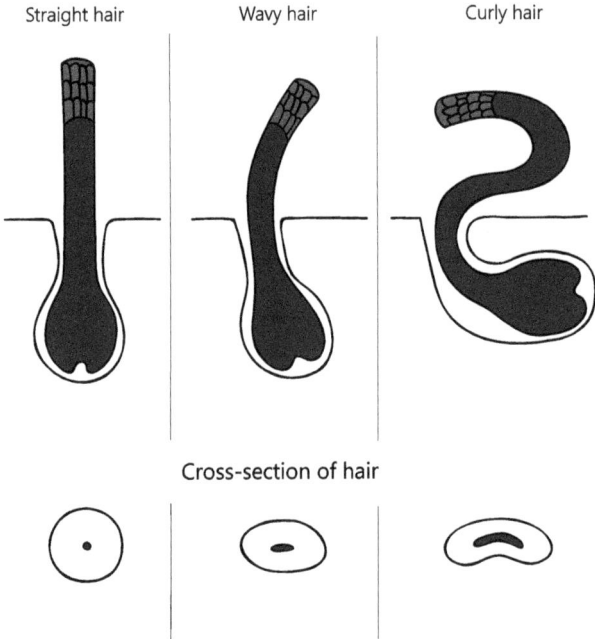

| Straight hair | Wavy hair | Curly hair |

Cross-section of hair

The structure of our hair is shown here in this graphic as it grows from beneath the scalp. Notice how it changes from straight to wavy to curly shapes. As the hair grows, it gets older. The ends of your hair that are below shoulder length are probably at least two or three years old depending on how fast your hair grows.

In addition, it has been shampooed at least a hundred times or more and exposed to all kinds of environmental influences that may cause damage.

This is why intensive conditioning treatments are advised, especially for longer hair. Hair products come in many different formulations.

The following endorsements might sound like a commercial but I don't have any paid arrangement with the products I'm referring to. I just enjoy using them on my clients and myself and the results are remarkable.

Some of my favorite products to use are: "Tropical Elixir" a Shine Therapy from YHS Hair Care by Alan Benfield Bush, rich in minerals, proteins, vitamins and antioxidants. This magical formula protects the hair from color fading and damage. Adds shine that leaves the hair with a lustrously smooth finish. Activated to penetrate into the cortex while protecting the cuticle, cutting drying time. His new line of hair products are being formulated for YHS - "Your Haircare System" Alan also wrote the foreword in this book.

Another hair care line I enjoy is called, "Bloody Gorgeous" formulated by Jon English, a modern day apothecary with a complete line of hair care products. My favorites to use are the Restorative Infusion Treatment and Miraculous Finishing Gloss for anti-frizz and shine.

I also use Framesi "Color Lover" Shampoo and Conditioners for all hair types. There is Curl Define for curly hair, Volume Boost for fine hair and Smooth Shine for straight hair.

I also use Pravana Hair Care Products and Aveda Hair Care Products.

Horst Rechelbacher, the founder of Aveda products formulated natural and toxic-free products in the beauty industry. As an author, his knowledge contained in his books are worth their weight in gold. Horst is now in heaven styling all the angels' hair… *(1941 –2014)*

*Everything we put in and on our
bodies must be nutritious and safe.
- Horst Rechelbacher*

I suggest using products that are:

♥ Sulfate free – (detergents)
♥ Paraben free (wax)
♥ Sodium chloride free – (salt free)
♥ DEA free
Products that have:
♥ Powerful anti-aging properties
♥ Thermal & UV protectants
♥ Weightless
♥ Will not build up on hair

Washing your hair everyday with chlorinated water is not a good idea. A water filter for the shower is recommended and is affordable.

For showering, I suggest using a sarong wrapped on your head. You have seen them at beach shops. They are a long piece of cloth with a smooth surface you wear over your bathing suit. Wrap this piece of cloth around your head like a turban before showering the next day.

The cotton sarong is smoother than a towel, because towel fibers will abrasively open the cuticle layer of the hair and cause frizz.

Shower caps work too but trap moisture at the scalp. You would then need to run a blow dryer on low heat with a low airflow through your hair at the scalp to dry the moisture so it doesn't frizz your hair. Read the labels on products. If your hair is dry, it needs a moisturizing conditioner. If it is breaking off and damaged it needs protein. Sometimes both are needed.

Hair Loss
Hair loss could be from many factors including:

1. Crash dieting or change in diet
2. Taking medication or stopping a medication
3. Stress
4. Iron deficiency
5. Underactive thyroid
6. Hormonal imbalances

After an imbalance is treated the hair growth continues to be slow for a few months then returns to normal. Each strand of hair on the human body is at its own stage of development.

Once the cycle is complete, it restarts and a new strand of hair begins to form.

Let me illustrate with a graphic to help you further understand.

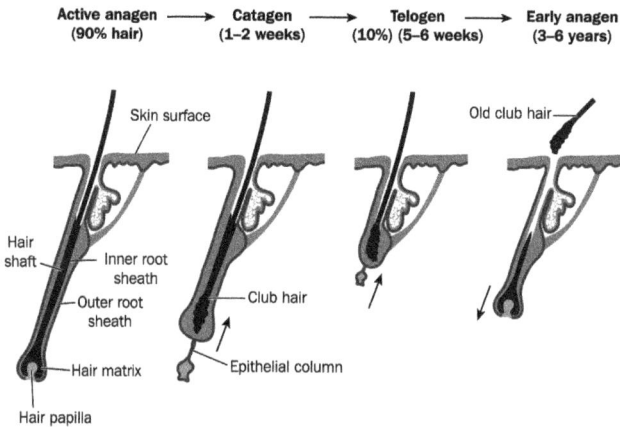

Hair grows in cycles of various phases: *anagen* is the growth phase; *catagen* is the phase where the hair falls out, known as the regressing phase; and *telogen* is the resting phase where it seems as though your hair is not growing. There is also a fourth stage called *exogyn*. On any given day, we lose about 50-150 scalp hairs due to *exogen*.

Looking at the graphic you will also see something called a "club hair". It's not from the club hair for men but when a new hair is formed and pushes the old club hair out. A club hair is one that has stopped growing or is no longer in the anagen phase. Scalp hair stays in this active phase of growth for two to six years.

Genetic hair loss is not marked by a rapid loss of hair. What actually happens is that shorter and finer hairs replace otherwise normal hairs until balding in areas may occur. It takes from ten to forty years for this process on the top or front of the hair as in a receding hairline or alopecia.

For women clients who give birth and then loose hair, it usually comes back as before. Sometimes the texture has changed. Some women losing hair take prenatal vitamins for a while in order to reverse this condition. Try not to stress if you are losing hair. Stress will only make it worse.

Some people have issues with frizzy hair. There are products you can use to help smooth your hair. There is something you can do on a regular basis to help reduce the frizz.

My client Stephanie asked me, "How do I stop the frizzies or frazzles on my hair right after washing?"

I asked her if she conditioned her hair and if she

rinsed it out really well? She said, "Yes, I rinse my hair for a long time because my hair gets oily from the conditioner." I asked her if she shampooed her hair once or twice while in the shower. She said, "Once."

I advised her to shampoo twice because the first shampoo gets the surface clean from the environment and the second gets the scalp clean.

I also explained to her that rinsing the conditioner too well could remove all of it, sending it's beneficial properties right down the drain.

I further explained how the conditioner helps to coat the hair and close the cuticle so the hair will reflect light and shine. Also, I told her to make sure to cool the water down before rinsing to help close the cuticle.

Then I asked Stephanie if she wrapped her head in a towel after her shower. She said, "Oh yes, I keep a towel on my hair for a while."

I told her to only wrap her wet hair in a towel while she dries off her body with a second towel, then immediately remove the towel on her hair and comb it out. I explained that the towel fibers cause the cuticle layer to open and cause her hair to be frizzy.

Two days later she sent me a text that said, "I took your advice, I didn't over-rinse the conditioner and I only put my hair up in a towel for a couple minutes and guess what? It worked! I was actually able to dry my hair after the shower and it didn't frizz up!

When hair gets frizzy it's because the cuticle is open or may be damaged.

I like to tell my clients:

"Rinse the conditioner from your hair then turn around in the shower and rinse off your hands. Then run your hands over your hair and it should feel soft and silky.

If you notice there is excess conditioner on your hands after doing this, rinse your hair again lightly. If you don't feel excess conditioner on your hands, stop rinsing.

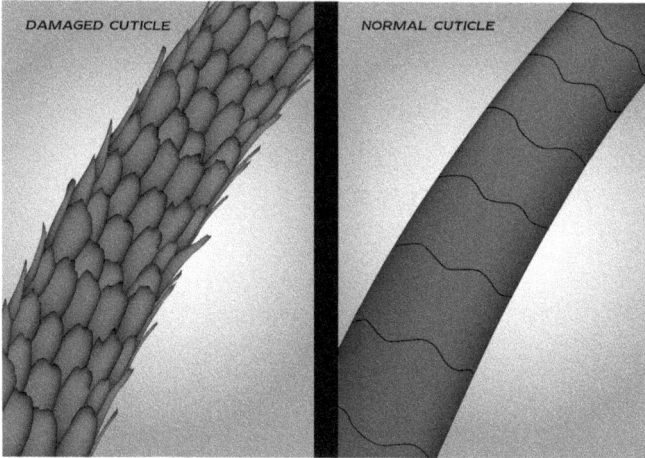
DAMAGED CUTICLE   NORMAL CUTICLE

An open damaged cuticle can result from not using a hair conditioner, by over use of chemicals, overexposure to sunlight, swimming in a chlorinated pool, sea salt in the ocean and/or inferior hair products that are too alkaline for the hair causing damage. A damaged cuticle layer can be somewhat restored with intensive treatments. Fortunately the hair grows fast enough to replace the damaged hair with healthy new hair.

About ninety percent of clients cannot remember what they use on their hair. I recommend that you learn the names of the products you presently use.

Some people use baby shampoo thinking it is gentle

on their hair. Baby shampoo is formulated to cleanse baby oil from a baby's scalp, it is higher in alkaline. The products you may be using on your hair may be high in alkaline leaving your hair cuticle wide open.

Split End

Clients ask me why getting their hair trimmed to get rid of split ends helps hair to grow longer. Looking at this graphic of a split end helps one to understand that when the split ends are trimmed, it prevents the ends of the hair from splitting further up the hair strand causing breakage.

Body Waves

Body waves give volume to hair for people with thin or flat hair and the wave or curls will depend on the size of the rod used to roll the hair and the direction they are placed on the head. There are various types of curl formation in body waves and perms.

A popular type is the spiral perm, created by using long perm rods or placing larger rods diagonally and wrapping the hair in smaller sections.

Then there is the designer body wave or perm called a "multi-textured perm". By using two or three different sized perm rods to form the curls, the wave formation ends up in varying sizes creating a more natural look.

Then there is the root perm that's great for fine, thin and lifeless hair. This process involves perming just the roots giving it volume. Root perms can be used on clients with who simply want to bring a bit of volume and texture to their hairstyle.

One type of perm that is coming back in style is the stacked perm. It is better for hair that is one length as opposed to shorter or longer hair with layers due to the fact that the hair is set on large rods only at the ends, giving the hairstyle more volume.

How are perms and body waves created?

This may be more than you ever really wanted to know, if you do, carry on …

We must first understand what holds hair together. About 95% of hair is a single keratin protein, which has a long helical shape.

A section of hair is wound around the chosen rod size and the first solution called waving lotion is applied to the top and underside of each and every rod. A chemical reaction takes place resulting in the hair taking on the shape of the rod.

The waving lotion is then rinsed off the hair for five full minutes and then towel blotted. The next step is to apply the neutralizer. The neutralizer sets the new shape of the hair. The rollers are carefully removed and the hair is then rinsed in warm water for three to five minutes.

I recently discovered a permanent wave product called Trionics, a chemical free and damage free perming solution with excellent results.

This new formulation actually leaves your hair with a fresh, clean fragrance. Yes, it's true no more going home with an awful perm odor.

Smoothing and Straightening Treatments

First of all, I suggest a natural smoothing treatment free of formaldehyde. Request one with natural ingredients formulated with enzymes and amino acids. It will modify the structure of curly or frizzy textures and smooth out your hair with shine and fullness.

There are products available that your Hair Designer can use to temporarily alter the curly, frizzy internal textural memory of the hair fiber transforming it into a sleek, smooth manageable condition. If you have curly hair and would like to choose a straight look, you will need a smoothing treatment.

Other factors to take into consideration are hairlines and growth patterns like cowlicks and whorls.

A whorl or cowlick

A whorl is located in the front hairline; a cowlick is at the crown on the top of your head, like a cow licked your head from the back.

Just so you understand, smoothing treatments only last about ten to twelve weeks, although some clients say they last about six months for them.

As the hair grows, it goes back to the original growth pattern and the cowlicks and whorls will reappear.

Smoothing treatments are a great choice for a special event like a wedding or a photo shoot. My favorite hair smoothing treatment product is Perfection SmoothOut™. Perfection's low pH formula contains no harsh chemicals such as formaldehyde, ammonium thioglycolate or sodium hydroxide that are found in traditional straighteners.

Pravana also has a Keratin product for straightening hair. One that gently but effectively transforms the internal bonds of the hair and simultaneously imparts pure keratin protein to both the interior and exterior of the hair shaft.

In my experience Pravana smoothing and straightening treatments are the best on the market.

Chapter 8
Inner Beauty

As within...

Beauty that comes from within is the only kind that will last. So how does one have inner beauty that lasts though the years? By having a heart that loves and understands, a heart and mind that forgives without keeping a record of wrongs.

By having faith and believing that they were born with a purpose, realizing what that purpose is and fulfills it. One who has confidence, the kind of confidence that does not compare how they look or what they may or may not have with other people. Maintaining beauty doesn't start with the hair.

Undeniable Beauty is perceived and appreciated by all of us. It is how humans are "wired". Here are some helpful observations to share with you...

Watch out for these often overlooked "basics" that can undermine your desire to present the Inner Beauty that is YOU.

Being competitive or jealous breeds anger, shame and guilt that can rob one of their inner beauty and peace.

The media does a great job of instilling these worthless values in the general public through advertisements, TV and movies. If competition only existed in sports I think life would be much sweeter.

As far as music and art, I believe it's considered to be subjective. The discoveries in science are always new and theories have to be proven to be fact. The kind of inner beauty I want to tell you about is the kind that gives you peace and does not entertain thoughts of fear and negativity.

Be *mindful* of what *occupies* your *mind*.

I like reading books on philosophy, psychology and religion. I own books I can learn from and share my knowledge with others to help their understanding in human relationships. What an opportunity to share wisdom and knowledge while I have a client sitting in my chair at the salon for an hour or two while I beautify them.

For me the most important thing in the world is Love. A child is born with innocence and learns what they live. DNA generates many factors in a personality but can be artfully molded into the beauty of patience, caring and truth.

A loving spirit can change the temperature in a room and create waves of positive energy. I always say, "You can steal my parking place but not my joy".

So how do you overlook the negativity you feel when confronted with the person looking you up and down in the grocery line or the relative that has a way to push your buttons and upset you, stealing your joy?

115

No one is perfect and there will be times when your armor is down and you get attacked or confronted without warning and react in a less than caring way. Forgive yourself and the other person and move on from it.

"The beauty of a woman must be seen from in her eyes, because that is the doorway to her heart, the place where love resides."
- Audrey Hepburn

Here is what I have learned and share with others.

I taught singing, film acting and image classes on weekends for eight years at John Robert Powers School in San Jose, California.

I learned some valuable lessons myself through teaching.

Be *mindful* of what *occupies* your *emotional* body!

When acting on film where the actor's head on the big movie screen is as big as a table revealing their every emotion on their face, one can see what they are thinking vividly. When teaching acting and observing the students rehearse the same lines again and again and then performing for the camera for the final filming, the actor learns to perform as if it is the very first time they have ever heard the dialogue in the scene. They have to make it appear as real, as if it is happening right now for the first time and react or respond to make it believable.

You and I have our favorite actors because they deliver a great, convincing performance and live the scene. The actor has to make a choice to either react or respond in order to be authentic in the scene. In life we should only react when it is an emergency or a surprise. People who react right away in most situations are lacking adequate control of their emotions.

A response is when one stops to think about what they want to say or do *before* they act on it. What does this have to do with inner beauty? A lot... when you have control over your emotions and you don't allow others to control you, life is good, and one's Inner Beauty can be most freely and sincerely expressed.

For instance, if someone asks you a question or requests that you do something for him or her and you are not sure if you can or how you feel about it… it's fine to say, "Let me think about it; I promise I will get back to you", or …"Hmm, let me sleep on it, I will let you know".

Unless it is an emergency, you can take the time you need because no one has the right to make you answer or respond unless you choose to. You don't have to give an answer unless you can be sure it is the right answer for you and the situation. This helps a lot in dating, marriage, family and your work environment as well.

And perhaps most importantly, the biggest enemies we have are fear, self-consciousness and feeling sorry for ourselves. Life is too short.

Many people live in fear and don't even know it. It filters everything we do and say. Fear is the tenant in the basement of our body, temple or house and rules the rest of the rooms in a figurative sense. Just as the brain connects to all parts of our bodies, fear can work through you unnoticed, you accept how you feel, thinking, "This is just the way I am…"

Many have said, "I can't help it." But I am here to tell you: Yes you can.

The tenants of fear are anger, guilt, shame, worry, anxiety, doubt, self-sabotage and I am sure you can think of one or two more.

In order to truly allow perceivable expression of our Inner Beauty, we have to evict fear and move in new feelings. It is impossible to be an empty shell.

We have to replace the negativity with positive, loving thoughts. Our negative thoughts have to be taken captive and replaced.

Have you ever been taking a shower and thinking thoughts about a potentially harmful situation and random thoughts come in that are something you would never say out loud to the person your are upset with …but there you are, finding yourself in a scene in reality saying the very thing you thought would never come out of your mouth… you just blurt it out with no control?

Trust me, if you think the same thought enough times you will eventually say it - and believe it.

At the risk of sounding a bit "scientific" about my approach to conveying the importance of this last chapter, I'll reference a quote from one of history's most notable and influential people in reference to his belief system and how "cause and effect" play out in our everyday lives:

"Anyone who becomes seriously involved in the pursuit of science becomes convinced that there is a spirit manifest in the laws of the universe... a spirit vastly superior to that of man"
- Albert Einstein

Only God can renew your mind. All the positive thinking on your own is still making you the God of your own heart, mind and soul.

When negative thoughts come in, take them captive and throw them out replacing them with a loving thought, a forgiving thought. Think and recall the foundation of "Inner Beauty".

Did you know that to have compassion for another person is as simple as being kind?

Our brains create new baby neurons every morning and it's the time to pray, plan and be grateful, no matter what your circumstances are, it could always be worse.

We have to learn from our mistakes and be careful not to judge others. If we do judge others we may find ourselves in the same exact situation five or ten years from now.

It's ok to witness and see things in order to help a situation and to pray, but having the habit of judging people unless you get paid for it like Judge Judy can be a tricky thing.

Inner beauty has qualities that shine like a light with a tranquil countenance. Someone who has mastered the expression of their inner beauty has no jealousy and can promote a desire from others who want to be around them because they feel acknowledged and appreciated.

To be filled with inner beauty means to move and act in love, peace, patience, kindness, forbearance, perseverance, forgiveness and mercy.

There will be moments and sometimes hours or days when stress and the actions of others will affect you deeply.

There may be people who take unjustified advantage of your kindness and project their negative or guilty feelings towards you to make you feel bad. This too shall pass.

You can forgive and make an executive decision to stay away from people who hurt your feelings. The only real things that change in life under our own power are the people we associate with and the books we read.

In a nutshell it's all about who you know and what you know.

There will also be times of loss and grieving. Loss of loved ones is natural and it seems when someone you love passes away, it brings up sad feelings of those you love that have passed on, left or abandoned you.

Although it may be difficult, try to stay grateful for the good memories and the time you had with them.

Remember that gratefulness and fear cannot co-exist. You are either living in one or the other.

Let your light shine from within you; let your love glow from your heart and through your eyes and... Rejoice in the expression and perfection of your own Inner Beauty. You will see the world with a different perspective.

Keep your eyes and thoughts lifted upwards with hope and faith that things will work out even when they look like they might not.

Every day is a new day. Do what you can to help someone, find your purpose and make a difference in someone's life. It will help make a difference in yours.

Be sure to ask God for his guidance and your angels to protect you. Be blessed and dazzle the people around you with love and gratitude.

"Gratitude is the memory of the heart."
- Jean Baptiste Massieu

Chapter 9
Terms and Definitions

Since I've emphasized the importance of proper and accurate terminology, the following is a collection from the "short list" to empower you to communicate successfully with your Hair Designer.

You may hear your Hair Designer mention some of these terms as your hair is being cut. Some definitions may be over your head but I'm here to educate and enlighten you. Here are the rest of the haircutting terms I wanted to share with you I regard as Hair Lingo.

Perimeter Line
Design line of a hairstyle used as a guide to a style where hair is trimmed at the ends in a V shape, a square shape, a convex shape or concave shape.

Sections
Hair divided and parted into uniform working areas for control.

Scissor-over-comb
A haircutting technique in which the hair is held in place with a comb while the tips of the scissors is used to remove the lengths.

Slicing
A technique that removes bulk and adds movement through the lengths of the hair; the shears are not completely closed, and only the portion of the blades near the pivot is used.

Slide cutting
A cool method of cutting hair where the scissors glide along the hair to remove length and keep weight at the perimeter. I love this technique!

Slithering

A process of thinning the hair to gradated lengths with shears; cutting the hair with sliding movement of the shears while keeping the blades partially opened.

Tapering

A haircutting effect in which there is even blending from very short at the hairline to longer lengths as you move up the head. To "taper" is to narrow progressively at one end.

Tension

The amount of pressure applied when combing and holding a section, created by stretching or pulling the section. When cutting wavy or curly hair, even tension is important for the best cuts.

Texturizing

A technique applied for removing excess bulk (volume) without shortening the length; changing the appearance through specific haircutting techniques, using shears or thinning shears. Also there are techniques for *increasing* volume.

Hair Color Terms:
There are different techniques for hair color to understand and for artistic effects. Here are some techniques and terms:

Balayage and free-form technique
Painting a lightener with an angled brush directly onto clean, styled hair or hair that has been colored at the root and then brought through free style by the hair colorist eyeing the amount brought through for a natural effect.

Base color
The natural predominant hair color level, color tone, intensity and base color.

Color fillers
Used when hair has been over processed. It is needed to equalize porosity and deposit color in one application to provide a uniform contributing pigment on pre-lightened hair. If hair has been damaged it may not hold color and wash right out.

Conditioner fillers
Used to recondition damaged, overly porous hair, and equalize porosity so that the hair accepts the

color evenly from strand to strand and scalp to ends. Protein and moisture need to be replenished when hair has been over processed or damaged from the environment. Hair damaged from salt water or chlorine can benefit from this treatment.

Demi-permanent hair color

Also called no-lift, deposit-only color. Formulated to deposit, but not lift (lighten) natural hair color. Demi-permanent colors are able to deposit without lifting because they are less alkaline than permanent colors and are mixed with a low-volume developer.

Developer

An oxidizing agent mixed with hair color, it supplies the necessary oxygen gas to develop color molecules to cause a change in hair color.

Developers most used in hair color are from a *five* volume to a *forty* volume and all in-between. Anything over a forty-volume developer could be dangerous.

Double-process application

A coloring technique requiring two separate procedures, in which the hair is pre-lightened with bleach before the depositing color is applied, also called two-step coloring.

Foil highlights or lowlights
A highlighting technique that involves coloring selected strands of hair by slicing or weaving out sections and applying lightener or permanent hair color, and sealing them in the foil or plastic wrap.

Glaze
A non-ammonia color that adds shine and tone to the hair. My favorite is, "Eclectic" by Framesi. It has a glaze formula made from sugar derivatives and gives hair a beautiful shine.

Hair Color Level
The level of lightness or darkness of hair color. Refers to the saturation, concentration, or density of a color. Hair color levels go from (level one being the darkest as in black hair) to (level eleven being the lightest blonde color) and some hair color lines go to a level twelve as their ultra light blonde.

Metallic hair color
Hair colors containing metal salts that change hair color gradually by progressive build-up and

exposure to air, create a dull, metallic appearance. You do not want this kind of color!

A lot of drug store and supermarket products contain these ingredients and I've had more than a few clients come to me with this kind of damage. What needs to be understood is that hair color products and hair sprays have polyvinyl chlorides (PVC's) used to make vinyl records and other petrochemical derived toxins and synthetic chemical aromatics.

Off the scalp lighteners
Powdered lighteners that cannot be used directly on the scalp or they could burn your scalp.

On the scalp lighteners
Oil and cream lighteners that can be used directly on the scalp and are gentler.

Patch test
A patch test is for identifying a possible allergic reaction for those who are sensitive to products.

Permanent hair colors
Lighten and deposit color at the same time and in

one application.

Pre-lightening
The first step of double process hair color. Bleach is used to lift or lighten the natural pigment before the application of a toner.

Resistant
Referred to as some hair types that make penetration by moisture or chemicals difficult.

Reverse highlighting or lowlighting
A technique of coloring strands of hair darker than the natural color.

Semi-permanent hair color
Is a depositing hair color formula that is for those who get their hair done once a week and the color lasts about 4 weeks. If you shampoo more often it will only last a couple of weeks.

Slicing
Coloring technique that involves taking a narrow, 1/8-inch section of hair, making a straight part at the scalp, then positioning the hair over the foil and applying lightener or color.

Soap cap

Combination of equal parts of hair color and shampoo applied to the hair like a regular shampoo.

Special effects hair coloring

A hair color technique that involves partial lightening or coloring in an artistic style.

Temporary hair color

Nonpermanent color whose large pigment molecules prevent penetration of the cuticle layer, allowing only a coating action that may be removed by shampoo.

Toner

A color formula mixed with a low volume developer that is used primarily on pre-lightened hair, to achieve pale and delicate colors.

Here are the shades of toners:

ASH (Cool) - has no red or gold highlights/tones (will minimize red/gold/brassy tones)
NEUTRAL - has an equal amount of primary colors (balanced)

BEIGE & CHAMPAGNE - similar to a neutral, but may be more warm or cool depending on base

GOLD (Warm) - color adds golden highlights/tones

RED (Warm) - color adds red highlights/tones

Virgin application
Is for virgin hair that's never been colored... ever.

This may be more than you ever wanted to know but perhaps you like reading the dictionary and are a perpetual student like me.

I like to know the *how* and *why*... about most things. I want to thank you for allowing me to share this journey with you thus far

I'm considering writing a second book, "Frazzle to Dazzle II" with even more to learn and more of *your* stories.

About the Author

Tricia Greenwood is a passionate Hair Designer, Color Specialist and Make-up Artist who is currently based in San Jose, California.

Hailing from Buffalo, New York, her passion for beautifying and helping people began early on and it has stayed with her ever since.

Throughout the span of over three decades, Tricia has been licensed in three states from New York to Houston, TX to California with clients ranging from models and musicians to stay-at-home Moms and Fortune 500 CEO's.

Her work has been featured in fashion shows, music videos and company photo shoots that display her artistic talent in helping a multitude of clients feel confident, vibrant, and uniquely beautiful.

As a seasoned Hair Designer who truly cares about her valued clients, she ensures that each and every product she uses is chemical free.

Hair Designing isn't simply a profession to her. It's a calling.

As an award winning, inspired beauty professional, Tricia's unrelenting quest for excellence has resulted in an unsurpassed wealth of knowledge regarding the beauty industry.

"For with God nothing will be impossible."
Luke 1:37